Do Not Disturb
·H·H·

DO NOT
DISTURB
ME,
EITHER!

In the Forest of Nod
by a slumbering stream,
there's a tall, twisting tree
that grew out of a dream.
Down through its branches,
silently oozing,
slides a slow, sleepy Snail
disturbed from her snoozing!

One Odd Old Owl,
in slumber so deep,
is snoring so loudly
the snail cannot sleep.

3

If there's one thing snails hate,
it's the sound of loud snoring.
So, spying two birds,
she at once starts imploring,
"Please, wake up that Owl.
It's time he was gone.
I want some sleep,
but he snores on and on!"

So . . . .
Two lazy Lovebirds
chirp, chirrup and cheep.
But One Odd Old Owl
continues to sleep.

"Louder," begs the Snail.
"Much more noise, if you please!"

So . . .
Three wily Woodpeckers
hammer harshly on the trees.
Two lazy Lovebirds
chirp, chirrup and cheep.
But One Odd Old Owl
continues to sleep.

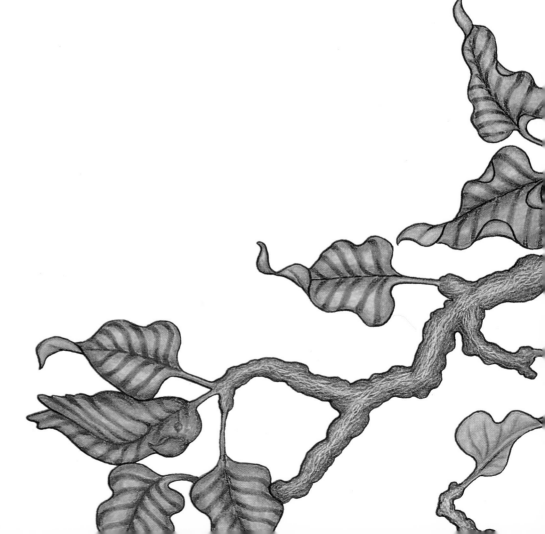

Then . . .
Four fine-feathered Flamingos
noisily knock their knees.
Three wily Woodpeckers
hammer harshly on the trees.
Two lazy Lovebirds
chirp, chirrup and cheep.
But One Odd Old Owl
continues to sleep.

"Louder," groans the Snail.
"The sun has almost set!"

So . . .
Five delightful Ducks
quack quickly in quintet.
Four fine-feathered Flamingos
noisily knock their knees.
Three wily Woodpeckers
hammer harshly on the trees.
Two lazy Lovebirds
chirp, chirrup and cheep.
But One Odd Old Owl
continues to sleep.

Then . . .
Six Canaries sing in chorus,
their song the sweetest yet.
Five delightful Ducks
quack quickly in quintet.
Four fine-feathered Flamingos
noisily knock their knees.
Three wily Woodpeckers
hammer harshly on the trees.
Two lazy Lovebirds
chirp, chirrup and cheep.
But One Odd Old Owl
continues to sleep.

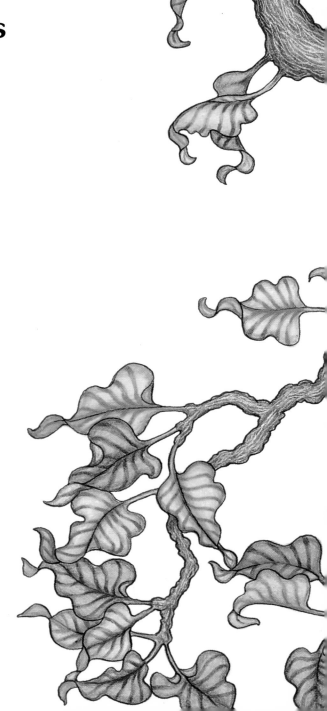

13

"Louder," cries the Snail.
"Or else he'll snore all night!"

So . . .
Seven harmonious Hummingbirds
whirr their wings in flight.
Six Canaries sing in chorus,
their song the sweetest yet.
Five delightful Ducks
quack quickly in quintet.
Four fine-feathered Flamingos
noisily knock their knees.
Three wily Woodpeckers
hammer harshly on the trees.
Two lazy Lovebirds
chirp, chirrup and cheep.
But One Odd Old Owl
continues to sleep.

Then . . .
Eight excited Parrots
screech and squawk with all their might.
Seven harmonious Hummingbirds
whirr their wings in flight.
Six Canaries sing in chorus,
their song the sweetest yet.
Five delightful Ducks
quack quickly in quintet.
Four fine-feathered Flamingos
noisily knock their knees.
Three wily Woodpeckers
hammer harshly on the trees.
Two lazy Lovebirds
chirp, chirrup and cheep.
But One Odd Old Owl
continues to sleep.

"LOUDER!" weeps the Snail, "If not,
he'll snore for weeks and weeks!"

So . . .
Nine crazy Cockatoos
shout in shrill, sharp shrieks.
Eight excited Parrots
screech and squawk with all their might.
Seven harmonious Hummingbirds
whirr their wings in flight.
Six Canaries sing in chorus,
their song the sweetest yet.
Five delightful Ducks
quack quickly in quintet.
Four fine-feathered Flamingos
noisily knock their knees.
Three wily Woodpeckers
hammer harshly on the trees.
Two lazy Lovebirds
chirp, chirrup and cheep.
But One Odd Old Owl
continues to sleep.

Then . . .
Ten tired Toucans
clitter-clatter bold, bright beaks.
Nine crazy Cockatoos
shout in shrill, sharp shrieks.
Eight excited Parrots
screech and squawk with all their might.
Seven harmonious Hummingbirds
whirr their wings in flight.
Six Canaries sing in chorus,
their song the sweetest yet.
Five delightful Ducks
quack quickly in quintet.
Four fine-feathered Flamingos
noisily knock their knees.
Three wily Woodpeckers
hammer harshly on the trees.
Two lazy Lovebirds
chirp, chirrup and cheep.
But One Odd Old Owl
continues to sleep.

"He'll never wake up,"
sobs the Snail with a sigh.
"Perhaps I can help?"
asks a voice in reply.

Then . . .
Out of the forest,
when all hope seems to fail,
steps a Proud Princely Peacock
with shimmering tail.
He takes a deep breath
and throws back his head.
Then he lets out a scream
that anyone would dread!

The deafening noise
rings out round the skies.
One Odd Old Owl yawns,
then opens both eyes!
Soon, soft, silent wings
through the starlight will soar.
"At last!" laughs the Snail.
"I can't hear that Owl snore!"

But before that poor Snail can ooze off to bed,

fifty-five birds start snoring instead!

The Snail stayed awake, while all the birds snoozed.
She grew rather cross and said, "I am not amused!
What else can I do that will help me to sleep?
I'll count all those birds. (I don't like to count sheep)."
But some of the birds were rather unfair.
They are cunningly hidden. Can you see where?

The Snail, wide awake, made up a new game.
"I'll hide all the letters that spell each bird's name.
That's fifty-six names to search for and spell.
And then, if you're clever, find *my* name as well!"

"Now when you've discovered everyone's name,
write down each last letter to play one more game.
The bird symbols hint where the letters should go.
If you get them right, my secret you'll know!"

Yours Puzzlingly,

The Insomniac Snail!

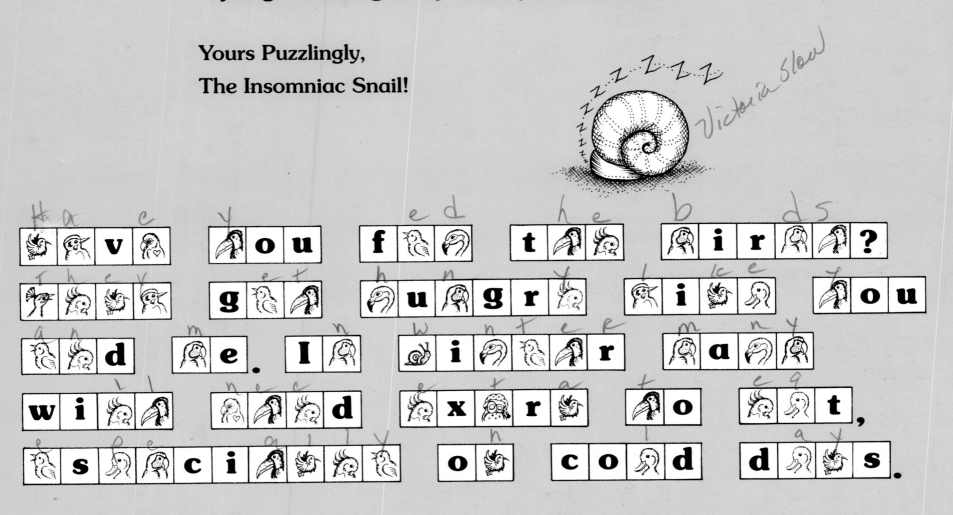

HINTS:

1. Starting on page 7, did you find the hidden bird on each page? There are twelve hidden on page 21.

2. Can you decode the peacock's secret message hidden in the feathers at the top left-hand corner of each page? The last feather is on the right-hand page.

3. The peacock says, "Good night, Sleep tight,..." Can you find the rest of his message on page 24?

For older puzzlers:

4. Each bird and the snail have a name hidden in the pictures — be clever and decode all 57! The letters are hidden one letter at a time (except for cockatoos and toucans), in correct order, whenever the individual bird appears. Make sure you are looking at the correct bird, they are all a tiny bit different. Use this chart over and over to help you fill in the letters you find. For repeated use, photocopy this chart before using, or write answers on a piece of tracing paper placed over the chart.

5. Use the last letters of each of the names on the chart to to fill in the missing letters of the snail's message on the last page. Use each bird only once.

TOUCANS (found on page 21)

_____

_____

_____

_____

_____

_____

_____

_____

_____

		PAGE NUMBERS											
		2/3	4/5	6/7	8/9	10/11	12/13	14/15	16/17	18/19	20/21	22/23	24/25
	Snail												
	Owl												■
LOVEBIRDS	Blue Eyelid	■										■	■
	No Eyelid	■		■								■	■
WOOD-PECKERS	Red Crest	■	■									■	■
	Orange Crest	■	■		■							■	■
	Dark Red Crest	■	■									■	■
FLAMINGOS	Green Eyes	■	■	■								■	■
	Pink Eyes	■	■									■	■
	Gold Eyes	■	■									■	■
	Blue Eyes	■	■			■						■	■
DUCKS	Curly Tail/Orange Feet	■			■							■	■
	Plain Tail/Orange Feet	■	■									■	■
	Curly Tail/Gold Feet	■	■									■	■
	Plain Tail/Gold Feet	■	■									■	■
	Plain Tail/Yellow Feet	■	■				■					■	■
CANARIES	Tan	■										■	■
	Orange	■	■									■	■
	Yellow	■	■									■	■
	Cream	■	■									■	■
	Beige	■	■									■	■
	Gold	■	■					■				■	■

A	B	C	D	E	F	G	H	I	J	K	L	M	N	O	P	Q	R	S	T	U	V	W	X	Y	Z
1	2	3	4	5	6	7	8	9	10	11	12	13	14	15	16	17	18	19	20	21	22	23	24	25	26

PEACOCK (found on page 22 and 23)

Don't let the bed bugs bite—

PAGE NUMBERS

	2/3	4/5	6/7	8/9	10/11	12/13	14/15	16/17	18/19	20/21	22/23	24/25
HUMMINGBIRDS												
Purple	■	■	■	■	■	■					■	■
Lavender	■	■	■	■	■	■					■	■
Maroon	■	■	■	■	■	■					■	■
Blue	■	■	■	■	■	■					■	■
Pink	■	■	■	■	■	■					■	■
Orange	■	■	■	■	■	■					■	■
Dark Purple	■	■	■	■	■	■			■		■	■
PARROTS												
Blue-Green Tail/Red Head	■	■	■	■	■	■					■	■
Purple-Orange Tail/Purple Head	■	■	■	■	■	■					■	■
Blue-Green Tail/Purple Head	■	■	■	■	■	■					■	■
Yellow-Orange Tail/Blue Head	■	■	■	■	■	■					■	■
Purple-Blue Tail/Red Head	■	■	■	■	■	■					■	■
Purple-Blue Tail/Purple Head	■	■	■	■	■	■					■	■
Orange-Red Tail/Blue Head	■	■	■	■	■	■					■	■
Blue-Red Tail/Green Head	■	■	■	■	■	■					■	■

PAGE NUMBERS

	3–17		19					21			23	25
COCKATOOS												
Yellow	■	■									■	■
Blue	■	■									■	■
Red	■	■									■	■
Orange	■	■									■	■
Lavender	■	■									■	■
Purple	■	■					■				■	■
Light Pink	■	■									■	■
Maroon	■	■									■	■
Dark Pink	■	■				■	■				■	■

ANSWER KEY
(To decode, hold up to a mirror)

1. The bird missing on each page is one of the birds which just appeared on the page before.
Page 7 — lovebird is a nest forward.
Page 9 — woodpecker is the top right bottom left.
Page 10 — flamingo is a bottom left branch. flamingo's bottom.
Page 13 — duck is upside-down in a top-
Page 15 — canary is the gap in leaves to center cloud.
Page 17 — hummingbird is at the bottom of the owl's right.
Page 18 — parrot is a leaf to left-center the tree trunk.
Page 21 — 12 hidden birds are 3 canaries, 3 ducks, 4 parrots, 1 lovebird: 3 on the branch, 3 on bird's wings, and 3 on the toucan.

2. I like snails.

3. Message hidden in the peacock's feathers — Don't let the red bugs bite.

4. Birds and stars names:
Stars (letters in antennae): Victoria Stowe
Owl (letters on night cap): Horatio Hoot
Lovebirds (letters on branch near each bird except last letter which is on bird's body):
Katherine, Jonathan
Woodpeckers (letters on wood chips):
Rosemary, Patricia, Michael
Flamingos (numbers on knees represent letters, i.e. 1=A, 2=B, 3=C, and so on. according to the alphabet): Bernard,
Ducks (letters on feet or beak): Daniel, Deborah, Maureen, Duncan
Canaries (letters on bills): Laura, Janet, Sheila, Philip, Claire, Norma
Hummingbirds (letters in wings around wings): Jack, Judy, Jean, Bill, Vera, Noah, Eve
Parrots (number of dots on cheeks represent letters): Joe, Ron, Kim, Don, Jim, Ivy, Bob, Ed
Cockatoos (letters in head feathers): Pam, Basil, Joyce, Alice, Nancy, Erin, Keith, Olive, Rosie
Toucans (letters on beaks in mirror writing): Elsbeth, Dorothy, Abigail, Herbert, Christine, Margaret, Dennis, Barbara, Annette, Jenny, Irene, Steve, Julie, Tony
Peacock (letter on crest): Albert

5. Have you fed the birds? They get hungry like you and me, in winter warm will need extra to eat, especially on cold days.

*Note: All the last letters shown up on the last bird of each species on page 21.

ANSWER KEY